A Note to Pa

Dorling Kindersley Readers is a compelling new program for beginning readers, designed in conjunction with leading literacy experts, including Dr. Linda Gambrell, President of the National Reading Conference and past board member of the International Reading Association.

Beautiful illustrations and superb full-color photographs combine with engaging, easy-to-read stories to offer a fresh approach to each subject in the series. Each *Dorling Kindersley Reader* is guaranteed to capture a child's interest while developing his or her reading skills, general knowledge, and love of reading.

The four levels of *Dorling Kindersley Readers* are aimed at different reading abilities, enabling you to choose the books that are exactly right for your child:

Level 1 – Beginning to read
Level 2 – Beginning to read alone
Level 3 – Reading alone
Level 4 – Proficient readers

The "normal" age at which a child begins to read can be anywhere from three to eight years old, so these levels are intended only as a general guideline.

No matter which level you select, you can be sure that you are helping your child learn to read, then read to learn!

LONDON, NEW YORK, MUNICH
MELBOURNE and DELHI

Senior Editor Linda Esposito
Senior Art Editor
Diane Thistlethwaite
US Editor Regina Kahney
Production Melanie Dowland
Picture Researcher Andrea Sadler
Jacket Designer David Kersh
Illustrator Peter Dennis

Reading Consultant
Linda B. Gambrell, Ph.D.

First American Edition, 2000
4 6 8 10 9 7 5
Published in the United States by DK Publishing, Inc.
375 Hudson Street, New York, New York 10014
A Penguin Company

Copyright © 2000 Dorling Kindersley Limited, London

Published in Great Britain by Dorling Kindersley Limited.

Library of Congress Cataloging-in-Publication Data
Donkin, Andrew.
Bermuda Triangle / by Andrew Donkin. -- 1st American ed.
  p.   cm. -- (Dorling Kindersley readers. Level 3)
Summary: Explores the mysteries and legends associated with the
Bermuda Triangle, an area in the Atlantic Ocean bounded by
Bermuda, Florida, and Puerto Rico, where hundreds of boats and
planes have vanished.
ISBN 0-7894-5415-7 (pbk) ISBN 0-7894-5416-5 (hardcover)
1. Bermuda Triangle--Juvenile literature. [1. Bermuda Triangle.]
I. Title. II. Series.
G558.D66 2000
001.94--dc21
                                99-043643
                                      CIP
                                      AC

Color reproduction by Colourscan, Singapore
Printed and bound in China by L Rex

The publisher would like to thank the following for
their kind permission to reproduce their photographs:
Key: c=center; b=bottom; l=left; r=right; t=top
Aviation Picture Library: cover, 20–21 t; Mary Evans Picture Library:
37 bl, 45 br, 47 cl; Fortean Picture Library: 14 br; William M. Donato
47 br; John Frost Historical Newspapers: 17 b, 22 b, 23 t; The
Granger Collection, New York: 9 br; Hulton Getty: 22 cl; Frank Lane
Picture Agency: 45 tl; David Legg Collection: 38 bl; Moviestore
Collection: 46 br; Science Photo Library: J. G. Golden 44 cl;
Topham Picturepoint: 10 br, 25 tr.

All other images © Dorling Kindersley.
For further information see: www.dkimages.com

see our complete product line at

www.dk.com

Contents

DK DORLING KINDERSLEY *READERS*

READING **3** ALONE

BERMUDA TRIANGLE

Written by Andrew Donkin

DK PUBLISHING, INC.

Legend of the lost

An amazing 1,500 people have vanished in the Bermuda Triangle over the last fifty years. Without doubt, it is the strangest area of water in the world. The heart of the Triangle lies between Florida, Bermuda, and Puerto Rico.

Bermuda Triangle

1881: a ship is found drifting with no one onboard. What has happened to the crew?

How can the five navy aircraft of Flight 19 just vanish?

NORTH AMERICA

BERMUI

30°

Jacksonville
FLORIDA
Fort Lauderdale
Miami
GULF OF MEXICO
BAHAMAS
CUBA
JAMAICA
HISPANIOLA
PUERTO RICO
CENTRAL AMERICA
CARIBBEAN SEA
PACIFIC OCEAN
90°
SOUTH AMERICA

But its eerie effect stretches east into the Sargasso Sea and south to Barbados.

Boats vanish from its surface without a trace. Planes disappear from its skies. Compasses go haywire for no reason.

What can be happening? In this book you can read about some of the most famous cases, then decide for yourself ....

What strange force tries to capture the barge being towed by the Good News?

A weird underwater craft is on a collision course with a small boat. What can it be?

When a clear sky turns to an unearthly yellow, can the flying boat reach safety?

SARGASSO SEA

ATLANTIC OCEAN

BARBADOS

N
W   E
S

30°

The ships' graveyard

The Sargasso Sea has been feared by sailors for centuries. It is a peculiar area of calm ocean that lies east of the island of Bermuda. The sea takes its name from a strange red seaweed, called sargassum, that covers its surface.

Sailors terrified their fellow seamen by telling tales of a ships' graveyard within the Sargasso Sea.

Trapped by the seaweed and the lack of wind, ships are said to sail on for centuries – never to escape. They are manned by crews of skeletons, the flesh on their bones long since rotted away!

The legend of the Bermuda Triangle may well have begun with old sailors' stories like these. However, it was the more recent disappearances that really put the Triangle on the map.

The missing

DATE: AUGUST, 1881
PLACE: ATLANTIC OCEAN – SOUTH OF BERMUDA

The lookout scanned the horizon carefully. There was something out there, he was sure of it.

"Ship ahoy!" he finally shouted from high in the crow's nest of the *Ellen Austin*.

In the distance was another ship, a schooner. Its sails were raised, but something was wrong.

"Call Captain Gould," ordered the lookout. "I think we've got a drifter!"

Captain Gould came up onto the deck. He was captaining the *Ellen Austin* across the Atlantic on its voyage from England to Newfoundland. If the other ship was really adrift, then Gould could put a crew onboard to sail her to port, where he could claim a salvage fee.

Salvage money

In those days, if a ship was abandoned at sea, anyone finding her could sail her back to port and claim a payment, called salvage rights, in return for their trouble.

"Mr. Morgan," said the captain to his second-in-command, "put together a boarding party. Let's have a look."

Morgan and five crewmen boarded the ship. Everything was silent except for the eerie creaking of the ship's timbers.

"Ahoy there?" shouted Morgan.

The splash of waves against the ship's sides was his only answer.

Both lifeboats were still onboard. Down in the cabins, everything was neat and orderly. But there was no sign of the crew or passengers – no clue to where they had gone or why.

Mary Celeste mystery
The *Mary Celeste* was found abandoned in the Atlantic Ocean in 1872. The fate of her crew remains a mystery.

Walking around the ghost ship gave
Morgan the shivers. It was so quiet.
What had happened to everyone?

Captain Gould put Morgan in charge
of a crew to sail the ghost ship back to
the port of St. John's in Newfoundland.
It was a task that Morgan did not relish,
even if he got a generous slice of the
salvage fee once they got to port.
He didn't want command of a
ghost ship. It was bad luck.

The two ships set
sail side by side,
heading west.

A few hours after dusk, they sailed into a bank of thick white fog. Neither crew could see more than a few yards in any direction.

"We've lost sight of her!" shouted the lookout on the *Ellen Austin.*

"Keep on course. We'll find her in the morning," ordered Captain Gould.

When the sun rose next morning, the crew of the *Ellen Austin* began to worry.

Although they could see as far as the horizon, there was no sign of the other vessel with their shipmates onboard. It was as if it had sailed off the face of the Earth.

19th-century merchant ship

The *Ellen Austin* began searching the area. Lookouts on all sides of the ship kept careful watch for any sign of the schooner. Captain Gould paced the deck nervously as the hours ticked away.

"Captain! Ship ahead!" shouted the forward lookout. "It's the schooner!"

As the *Ellen Austin* got nearer, the captain anxiously scanned the deck for signs of life.

Vincent Gaddis

The phrase Bermuda Triangle was first used by writer Vincent Gaddis in *Invisible Horizons*, a book about true sea mysteries. He also called the area the Triangle of Death.

"Ahoy, Mr. Morgan!" he called.

There was no answer. This time Captain Gould himself boarded the ship. As he looked around, an icy chill ran down his spine. Morgan and his crew had vanished. There was no sign that they had even been onboard.

The captain ordered his men back to the *Ellen Austin*. They sailed away as quickly as they could. The ghost ship was abandoned once more to its lonely fate.

The vanishing of Flight 19

DATE: DECEMBER 5, 1945
PLACE: EAST OF FORT LAUDERDALE
NAVAL AIR STATION, FLORIDA

"Sir, you'd better come over to the control tower!" shouted the young ensign. "Flight 19 is in trouble!"

Lieutenant Kingston followed the ensign toward the control tower of the Naval Air Station. Inside, he found the air station's controller frantically trying to make radio contact with Flight 19.

"This is an emergency. We seem to be off course," the voice of Charles Taylor, Flight 19's leader, crackled over the radio.

Kingston couldn't understand it. The five Avenger torpedo bombers had taken off on a training mission earlier that day.

The weather was good. All five planes had performed the practice bombing run without a hitch. Then, on the flight back to the base, the pilots had suddenly reported that their instruments were going crazy.

Now Flight 19 was in real danger.

Avenger torpedo bombers

Charles Taylor was scared. From the cockpit of his Avenger, the flight leader scanned the horizon. Just minutes ago, his compass had begun spinning in circles. It was difficult to work out where they were anymore, or where they should be heading. Nothing looked familiar.

He couldn't understand what was happening.

"Everything is wrong. Strange. We can't be sure of our direction," Taylor reported to the base. "Even the ocean doesn't look like it should."

Taylor strained to see if there was any sign of land ahead, but he could see none. He looked for the red ball of the setting sun. If he could find it, they could set their course by it and head back to the base. But there was nothing – no sun, no land … nothing.

Alarm was setting in among the staff in the control tower. How could the five planes become so lost when they were only 200 miles from base? Even worse, the radio signals were growing weaker and weaker, as if the planes were flying the wrong way. Most of their messages were being lost in static.

The control tower was full of people now, all anxious about their friends in the air. Suddenly, the radio burst into life once more.

"We are completely lost," said the voice of Taylor. "We're going to …" Then there was silence, a complete and chilling silence.

"Come in, Flight 19. Respond please," begged the controller. But there was no answer.

"Start an air-sea search immediately," ordered Lieutenant Kingston. "I want the entire area searched. Let's find those men!"

Nearly one hundred ships and planes took part in the search. But no trace of Flight 19 was found anywhere – not one life jacket or wreckage of any kind.

But that wasn't the end of the mystery.

A Martin Mariner aircraft that had been sent out as part of the search team failed to return to its base. The aircraft with 13 men onboard was never seen again. It vanished just like the planes it was searching for.

The riddle continues

In 1990, newspapers reported the discovery of Flight 19. But it was five similar planes that had been deliberately sunk a few years earlier.

Crew members of Flight 19 pictured at Fort Lauderdale

There have always been rumors of a final radio signal heard long after the planes vanished. The letters "FT … FT" were repeated several times, two hours after the planes would have run out of fuel. FT was the code sign of Flight 19. The signal seemed to come from nowhere and to echo away into the night.

Investigators have long argued about the cause of Flight 19's disappearance. Was it human error? Was it bad weather? Or was a far stranger force at work?

The fog

DATE: SPRING, 1966
PLACE: MID-VOYAGE BETWEEN PUERTO RICO
AND FLORIDA

The second officer looked across the bridge as, one by one, the instruments around him flickered and died. The ship's compass was spinning clockwise at an increasing speed.

"What's wrong?" demanded Captain Henry, as he climbed onto the bridge.

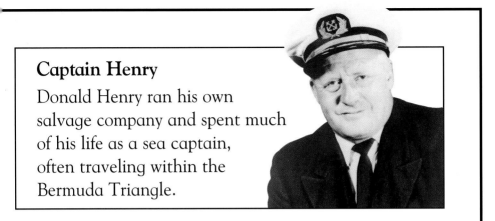

Captain Henry
Donald Henry ran his own salvage company and spent much of his life as a sea captain, often traveling within the Bermuda Triangle.

The 160-foot tug called the *Good News* was three days into a voyage from Puerto Rico to Fort Lauderdale, Florida. The *Good News* was towing a cargo barge behind her, attached by a strong line. The captain hadn't been expecting any problems and was surprised to be called to the bridge.

The second officer looked flustered. "The instruments just started going crazy," he explained. "Now, power is down on all the electrical equipment. I don't understand … it's like the power is being drained away by something!"

Captain Henry's first thoughts were for the safety of the cargo barge they were pulling. He looked outside – and couldn't believe what he saw.

A few moments ago it had been a perfectly clear day, but now the sky and the sea seemed to blur into a milky yellow haze. Henry could no longer make out the line of the horizon.

"What is it?" asked the second officer.

"Full ahead!" ordered Captain Henry. "Let's get moving." The men around him were becoming agitated. He could see fear in their eyes.

The ship's engines were slammed onto maximum power, but the tug did not move forward.

Up on deck, Captain Henry saw why.

Behind the *Good News,* a bank of thick, glowing fog covered the cargo barge. But there was no other fog anywhere else on the sea!

Where the fog touched the surface of the ocean, the water was choppy and rough, but Captain Henry could not understand what could be causing it.

He began to worry, not just for the barge, but for his own ship.

The captain felt that somehow the fog bank had hold of the barge and was refusing to let go. Worse, it was pulling them back toward it.

"Keep her on full power!" he shouted. He knew they had to get away, and soon.

For the next five minutes the *Good News* seemed to be locked in a battle with the bank of weird fog. The ship's engines pushed them forward, and then the fog pulled them back again ....

As the tug-of-war went on, the ship began to creak under the strain. Henry knew the legend of the Triangle. Were they about to become its latest victims?

With one final, mighty effort from its engines, the *Good News* lurched forward. Behind them, the cargo barge slipped out of the fog bank at last.

As they sailed to the safety of the nearest port, the crew members were unusually quiet. They had all heard tales of ships that had sailed into eerie fogs, never to be seen again. They knew they were lucky to be alive!

Collision course

DATE: APRIL, 1973
PLACE: NORTH OF MIAMI

It was a beautiful April afternoon, and Dan Delmonico was looking forward to a few hours of relaxing sailing. As he steered his small leisure boat out of Miami harbor, he had no idea that he was on a collision course with the unknown!

Just after four o'clock, Dan checked his compass reading and changed course slightly. With a smile of satisfaction, he watched the bow of his boat cut through the clear blue water.

Suddenly, he caught sight of something in the water ahead of him. Dan leaned over the side of his boat to get a better look.

He could scarcely believe what he saw.

Moving through the water was a long smooth craft. Dan had seen nothing like it in all his years on the ocean.

The strange craft was nearly 200 feet long and was moving at an incredible speed. Its surface seemed to be completely smooth. It had no windows or fins of any kind.

With a growing feeling of panic,
Dan realized that the craft was rising –
heading for the surface straight toward
his boat! It was moving too fast for Dan
to get out of the way. All he could do
was watch helplessly as the huge object
sped toward him. It looked as if the craft
would hit his boat and smash it to pieces.

At the last moment, the huge craft stopped rising toward the surface – as if it had spotted Dan's boat just in time.

The craft swiftly changed course and passed safely under Dan's boat. Then it disappeared, moving away into the depths of the Atlantic Ocean.

Some people have suggested that what Dan saw that day was a navy submarine. But Dan has always insisted that the thing he came so close to hitting was no submarine – at least, not one built by human hands.

Strange lights and unidentified craft have been reported by several witnesses in the Bermuda Triangle. Could these be behind some of the disappearances?

Official UFO
This UFO (Unidentified Flying object), seen flying toward an island in the Bermuda Triangle, was photographed by the Brazilian Navy.

Out of the blue

DATE: JUNE 11, 1986
PLACE: ON THE WAY TO JACKSONVILLE, FLORIDA

Of all the tales from the Triangle, perhaps the following story is the most extraordinary of them all.

In the summer of 1986, Martin Caidin, his wife, and five friends were piloting a Catalina (a flying boat) from England back to Florida. They were now on the last leg of their journey. The plane was equipped with the most modern flying instruments. It even had a satellite link.

Catalina
This large flying boat is a safe way of flying over the ocean because it can land on water if necessary.

The link enabled them to see photographs showing what the weather was like ahead of them.

The friends, several of whom were experienced pilots, were in good spirits and took turns guiding the plane through the perfect blue sky.

But suddenly, as Caidin stood behind the pilots in the cockpit, the whole world changed!

"What the heck just happened to the sky?" exclaimed Caidin.

No one could answer him. In an instant, the clear blue sky had changed to a milky yellow mess!

Then, one by one, the instruments in the cockpit began to fail. Caidin called for help on the radio, but all he got in reply was loud static.

"Even the satellite link is dead," Caidin reported to the others.

Outside, the yellow haze surrounded them in all directions.

But the strangest thing of all was a small wormhole that seemed to be keeping pace with the plane.

This narrow tunnel cut through the yellow mess so they could still see the ocean below. If they could just keep sight of the sea, they might not crash.

They flew on for an hour, trapped in
the ugly yellow sky ... then another
hour passed ... and another.

"Shall I take over for a while?"
offered Caidin. The friends were
taking turns in the two pilots' seats.
Flying in these conditions took all their
concentration. If they hadn't been so
experienced, they probably would have
crashed hours ago.

Then suddenly, without warning, they were flying in a clear blue sky again.

"I'll turn around," said Caidin. "Let's see what we've been flying through."

Caidin put the Catalina into a steep turn. Behind them, the sky was perfectly clear. There was not a single cloud.

"What on Earth was it?" Caidin asked.

Although they were all to ask the same question many times in the future, they never found the answer.

A natural explanation?

Some people do not believe there is anything strange about the Triangle. They suggest more down-to-earth reasons for some of the disappearances.

The area is known for its unpredictable weather. Sudden storms are common.

Waterspout in the Bermuda Triangle

A combination of freak weather conditions can create waterspouts. These travel at incredible speeds, destroying anything on the surface of the ocean or flying in the air above it.

Any wreckage that is left behind would be quickly swept away by the powerful currents of the Gulf Stream.

 A craft that sank just a few miles from the coast would be lost in more than 5,000 feet of water, making it almost impossible to find.

The misreading of compasses could also account for some of the vanishings. The Triangle is one of only two areas in the world where a magnetic compass points to the true north. This special condition makes it easy for people to become confused about where they are.

Columbus

When Christopher Columbus sailed through the Triangle on his voyages, he noticed that his compass was not working properly. But he did not tell his superstitious crew.

Out of this world

There are many bizarre theories about what could be going on. Many weird lights have been seen in the skies over the Triangle, and some researchers suggest that the area is a UFO hunting ground, where aliens from other worlds kidnap human beings.

Another suggestion is that the area is some kind of window linking this world with another dimension. Under certain conditions, things might slip from this reality into another. Reports do share odd features – like a merging of sea and sky.

The unXplained
The Bermuda Triangle has inspired many stories and films. This X-Files episode had Agent Mulder trapped on a marooned ship.

The loss of compass headings and radio contact reported by ships and planes has also been experienced by the space shuttle when flying over this area.

Perhaps the most offbeat idea is that the missing are being taken by Atlantians! The legend of Atlantis tells of a scientifically advanced city, which sank beneath the ocean in a massive flood thousands of years ago.

But, stranger still, the American faith healer Edgar Cayce (1877–1945) said that Atlantis would be found near the Bahamas in 1968. Submerged ruins were found as predicted.

Maybe one day soon the mystery will be solved.

Submerged road

Glossary

Atlantis
Legendary island that ancient stories say was destroyed in a terrible disaster.

Bermuda Triangle
An area of ocean in which dozens of ships and planes are said to have disappeared.

Bomber
A plane designed to drop bombs.

Bridge
The area of a ship containing its main controls where the captain and officers give their orders to the crew.

Cargo barge
Long, slow-moving vessel built to carry the maximum load.

Cockpit
The front section of an aircraft where the pilot sits surrounded by instruments.

Code sign
Code name used to tell one aircraft from another.

Compass
A device used to help ships and planes find out where they are.

Control tower
A building in which people give orders to aircraft landing and taking off.

Crow's nest
A position high in a ship's mast where a lookout has an excellent view.

Drifter
A ship that has been abandoned by its crew and is now carried along only by the ocean's winds and currents.

Ensign
A low-ranking officer in the navy.

Ghost ship
A supernatural vessel manned by ghosts.

Gulf Stream
Powerful ocean current that pushes warm water from the Gulf of Mexico across the Atlantic Ocean to Europe.

Salvage right
The right to claim an abandoned ship.

Sargassum
Unusual red seaweed that floats on the surface of the Sargasso Sea.

Schooner
A fast-moving sailing ship with two or more masts.

Tug
A powerful boat used for pulling or guiding larger ships.

UFO
Stands for "Unidentified Flying Object," a term often used to mean an alien spacecraft.